We Fought for Freedom

The Story of Our American Revolution

NEW
YORK

NEW
HAMPSHIRE

MASSACHUSETTS

Saratoga

→ Lexington & Concord
→ Boston (Bunker Hill)

RHODE
ISLAND

CONNECTICUT

PENNSYLVANIA

The Delaware River

→ New York & Brooklyn

Trenton ←
Valley Forge ←
Philadelphia ←

Monmouth

NEW JERSEY

DELAWARE

MARYLAND

VIRGINIA

→ Yorktown

→ Guilford
Courthouse

King's
Mountain ←

NORTH
CAROLINA

Cowpens ←

SOUTH
CAROLINA

→ Camden

Augusta

Charleston

GEORGIA

Savannah

N
W   E
S

American Colonies During the Revolution

Helpful Hint: Colonial boundaries don't always match today's state boundaries. For instance, West Virginia was still part of Virginia back then.

We Fought for Freedom

The Story of Our American Revolution

Tara Ross

Illustrated by

Kate E. Sands

COLONIAL PRESS, L.P.
Dallas, Texas
www.colonialpressonline.com

⭐ Acknowledgments ⭐

I owe a big "thank you" to so many teachers, parents, homeschoolers, and children from all over the country. It seems that each of my books ends up with its own review process. I printed and mailed hard copies wherever possible for *She Fought, Too* and *We Elect a President*, but that was impossible in 2022. Supply chain shortages moved up book deadlines and ensured that the review process for this book would need to be fully digitized. The Dropbox file I created ended up with a few dozen people collaborating and sending me feedback. Everyone gave me something new to think about, and I am so appreciative. To all of you who offered help, just for the love of history: Thank you, thank you. I hope you enjoy the final product.

COLONIAL PRESS, L.P.
6125 Luther Ln., No. 280
Dallas, Texas 75225
www.colonialpressonline.com

First Edition

ISBN: 978-0-9770722-5-5
Library of Congress Control Number: 2022938365

Printed in the United States of America

For Adam, Emma, and Grant,
with much love

Tara

To my husband, Victor, and our four
nephews, Braiden, Christopher, Oliver, and
Trey, with lots of love

Kate

⭐ A Note for Teachers and Parents ⭐

The story of our American Revolution can be difficult to teach to younger children. It's a long story that seems incompatible with their shorter attention spans. Despite this challenge, it's vital that younger generations know our heritage if we are to remain free. I hope the format of this book helps parents with this challenging task.

I've divided the Revolutionary War into 16 topics. Each topic has its own double-page spread, although the victory at Yorktown was important enough to earn four pages. Likewise, few realize that the Revolution in the South lasted for years: Our history books tend to discuss only the northern battles. Thus, the Revolution in the South also merited two double-page spreads.

My guess is that some children will read *We Fought for Freedom* in one sitting, but most won't. The structure of the book allows kids to move slower, perhaps choosing one topic per day as a bedtime story. Either way, I hope that separating the Revolution into bite-size portions will help children remember the general Revolutionary War timeline and how the war progressed. It seems so much easier than memorizing a timeline, although I've provided one of those at the end of the book, too.

More detail on any of these topics can be found in the index at the back of the book or in the "Fun Fact Corners" that appear in the main text. The back pages are aimed at parents, but older children may enjoy them, too.

I would be remiss if I didn't acknowledge that *We Fought for Freedom* focuses on the contributions of men. Most of the soldiers and delegates to the Continental Congress were men, so that's just how it works out. Having said that, women also helped in many important ways, but their contributions tended to be behind-the-scenes. Please check out my book, *She Fought, Too: Stories of Revolutionary War Heroines* for more on the contributions of women.

Last but not least, I must conclude with a special thank you to Kate Sands, my wonderful illustrator. Kate is the same artist who worked on *We Elect a President* and *She Fought, Too*. I feel blessed by the partnership and look forward to more projects. Thank you, Kate!

We both hope everyone enjoys our book.

Tara

★ Introduction ★

Where did the United States come from? Our country didn't always exist. We used to be part of Great Britain, a kingdom on the other side of the Atlantic Ocean.

Many of our great-great-great-great grandparents made a dangerous trip across the ocean to get here. They wanted to come to America so they could be free. They weren't always free in Great Britain because the King was too bossy.

Many were especially mad that the King tried to tell them what church to attend.

In America, they could make their own choices.

Back then, states were called colonies, and the people who lived in them were called colonists. The colonists built new homes and farmed the land. They created new cities. It was hard work, but they made a good life in America.

The colonists were still British citizens, and they were supposed to be treated the same as any other British person. But the people in Great Britain forgot what they were supposed to do. They quit caring about treating American colonists fairly. Instead, they got very bossy.

A war known as the American Revolution followed. It was difficult, but Americans fought because they wanted to be free. They knew that God gives everyone the right to life, liberty, and the pursuit of happiness. A King or Queen does not get to make choices for us.

Here is the story of how the United States of America began, and how we came to be free.

★ Great Britian Gets Bossy ★

Great Britain was not the only country to send colonists to America hundreds of years ago. Countries like France and Spain also sent people, but then everyone began fighting about who got which part of America. Great Britain spent a lot of money on these fights.

The British needed more money, so the British legislature, which is called Parliament, passed a law called the Stamp Act. The stamp wasn't to mail a letter, like it is today. It was a tax, paid when Americans bought stamps for their newspapers and legal documents.

The American colonists were very upset. They did not get to vote for the people in Parliament. Why should Parliament get to tax Americans?

Fun Fact Corner

- The French and Indian War was one early war fought over land in America.
- Parliament thought the taxes were fair: Shouldn't colonists pay for their own defense? The argument left out the other side: The size of the empire grew after the French and Indian War, which benefitted the King.
- Other tax measures passed and were controversial during this time, such as the Sugar Act (1764) and the Townshend Acts (1767-68).

To learn more about the Stamp Act, turn to page 43.

No one should be taxed unless they have a chance to vote for—or against—the government officials who are creating the taxes. Otherwise, government would take more and more money because no one could stop them. Americans used a simple phrase for this idea: "No taxation without representation!"

The colonists refused to obey Parliament. They did not buy the stamps. Many American women began weaving their own cloth so they could spend less money on British items. Others got stamp collectors to quit their jobs.

In the end, Parliament repealed the Stamp Act, which means Americans didn't have to pay that tax anymore.

Americans thought they had made their point, but Britain would find more excuses to be bossy after the Stamp Act.

★ The Boston Tea Party ★

The British government still wanted money. Parliament had gotten rid of the Stamp Act, but then it tried again. It created new taxes on things like paper, paint, and tea.

Americans were angry, so Parliament got rid of many of these taxes, too. Yet the tax on tea stayed. Then Parliament made things worse. It passed the Tea Act of 1773, which made it hard to buy tea from American suppliers. Parliament wanted Americans to buy tea from a British company instead.

One night, a ship full of British tea arrived in Boston. Two more ships followed. Now three ships full of tea sat in Boston Harbor, and taxes were due on all of it. The colonists did not want to pay these taxes, so a group called the Sons of Liberty came up with a plan.

More than 100 men disguised themselves as Mohawk Indians because they wanted everyone to know that they were Americans first, not British. These men boarded the ships in the middle of the night, and they threw all the tea into the water. They went home before anyone could figure out who they were.

When the King and Parliament found out what had happened, they were very upset. They decided to get even more bossy.

Fun Fact Corner
- An odd effect of the Tea Act was that it lowered the price of tea sold in America, but the Sons of Liberty knew cheaper tea could be a trick to make Americans accept the tax.
- The Boston Tea Party was orderly and organized. It was not an excuse to loot and steal. The Sons of Liberty did not destroy anything on the ships (except the tea). They even returned later to replace the single item that had been accidentally harmed: a padlock.

To learn more about the Boston Tea Party, turn to page 43.

★ Great Britian Punishes Boston ★

News traveled very slowly in 1773 because telephones and the Internet didn't exist yet. It was several weeks before Parliament learned of the Boston Tea Party, but when its members found out what Bostonians had done, they were very angry.

Parliament passed new laws to punish Boston. The port of Boston was closed. No more ships would be allowed in until Boston paid for the tea that had been destroyed. Parliament also made changes so that people in Massachusetts couldn't be in charge of their own government.

British soldiers were sent across the ocean to make sure that the colonists obeyed the new laws.

A committee in Boston sent letters to other colonies, asking for help. This was a big deal because each colony usually took care of itself, but now the colonies began working together. They sent representatives to a new type of meeting. It was called the Continental Congress.

That Congress organized a boycott of British goods. The members also signed a petition to the King, and they wrote a letter to Canada to see if Canadians would help.

The King ignored the petition. Things were about to get a lot worse.

Fun Fact Corner

- Parliament's new laws came to be known as the "Intolerable Acts."
- Georgia was the only colony that did not send delegates to Congress.
- Congress had to decide how to vote. The small colonies were afraid of being bullied by the big colonies, so it was agreed that each colony would get one vote.
- The delegates wanted to open with prayer, but they all had different religions. Who would pray? Samuel Adams said he'd join any "gentleman of piety and virtue, who was at the same time a friend to his country."
- Others agreed, and an Anglican clergyman opened Congress in prayer.

To learn more about the Intolerable Acts, turn to page 44.

★ Paul Revere's Midnight Ride ★

The colonists knew things were getting very bad, so they got their militia ready. Militia are like soldiers, but they aren't a regular army. They are just normal people trying to take care of their homes and communities.

The British still wanted to be bossy, but they knew it would be harder if Americans had guns. The militia stored guns and supplies in Concord, Massachusetts, so hundreds of British soldiers got ready to march there. They planned to take the militia's guns and ammunition.

On the way to Concord, the British would stop in a town called Lexington to arrest two important Sons of Liberty: Samuel Adams and John Hancock.

Fun Fact Corner

- Revere did not finish the ride to Concord because he was briefly captured by the British. A man named Samuel Prescott finished the ride instead.
- Sometimes people say that Paul Revere yelled, "The British are coming!" as he rode, but he didn't. He may have told people that the "redcoats are coming" or the "regulars are out!"

To learn more about Paul Revere's ride, turn to page 45.

Some Americans figured out the British plan. Another well-known Son of Liberty, a man named Paul Revere, got on his horse and rode towards Lexington and Concord in the middle of the night.

A second man named William Dawes also rode with the same warning, but he took a different road. If the British captured one of the men, then the other would still have a chance to get through.

Fortunately, both Dawes and Revere made it to Lexington. They warned Adams and Hancock about the soldiers coming to arrest them, then kept riding to Concord.

A big fight was going to start the next day!

✭ "The Shot Heard 'Round the World!" ✭

The morning after Paul Revere's ride, the British were still marching to get the guns and ammunition from Concord. They had made it as far as Lexington when they ran into 70 American militia.

The British marched towards the Americans, but the Americans would not back down. Someone heard a British soldier yell at the militia to put down their guns.

He said it rudely, calling Americans "rebels" and "villains."

No one is sure who fired the first shot, but someone did. A short fight followed, but the British got away and kept marching to Concord. Someone started a fire in Concord, and some Americans thought the British were trying to burn down the town. More militia came out to fight.

The British effort to get the militia's guns and supplies hadn't worked, so they began the long march back to Boston. Americans chased them the whole way.

Afterwards, the British were trapped in Boston with Americans surrounding the city. The American Revolution had begun!

Fun Fact Corner

- The first shot fired at Lexington is sometimes called "the shot heard 'round the world" because the effects of our Revolution would be felt worldwide.
- Some British thought the first shot was fired by a colonist hidden behind a bush or in a tavern, but many Americans were sure the British fired first.
- Both the American and British commanders at Lexington later said that they ordered their men not to fire, but many never heard the orders.

To learn more about Lexington and Concord, turn to page 46.

⭐ General George Washington ⭐

The British were trapped in Boston, and the American colonists realized that they would need to work together again. They sent delegates to another Continental Congress, just like they did after the Boston Tea Party.

Americans were entering a war against the British, which then had the most powerful army and navy in the world. No one thought Americans could win. They would need to build a new army, with a talented Commander-in-Chief.

Fun Fact Corner

- Washington served as Commander of the Virginia Regiment when he was just 23 years old. Later, he was a representative in Virginia's colonial government, which was called the House of Burgesses. He served in both Continental Congresses.
- After the war, Washington wrote that the "establishment of Civil and Religious Liberty was the Motive which induced me to the Field."
- The new American army was called the Continental Army.

To learn more about General George Washington, turn to page 47.

One of the congressional members from Massachusetts, John Adams, suggested that George Washington should lead the American army.

Washington was respected and known by everyone because of his service in previous wars and in Virginia's government. Adams thought that Washington would be able to convince soldiers from different colonies to work together.

Some people complained that the war was mostly in the North and Washington was from the South, but Adams convinced everyone that Washington was the best choice.

In the end, George Washington was appointed Commander-in-Chief of the new army. He left to join the American militia sitting outside Boston, but one important battle occurred before he could get there.

★ The Battle of Bunker Hill ★

The British were working on a plan to escape Boston and attack Americans. They'd been trapped for months, and they did not like it.

In the meantime, Americans had their own plan. They would build new defenses on Bunker Hill, near Boston. It would stop the British attack.

A militia officer named Colonel William Prescott was sent to put up these defenses. He and his men would work all night building walls and installing cannons.

The British would wake up to a big surprise!

Then something weird happened: Prescott made a mistake and fortified Breed's Hill instead of Bunker Hill. It was closer to Boston than intended.

Prescott also got started too late, so his men weren't done with the defenses when the sun came up. Prescott leapt onto a wall, right where the British could see him. He encouraged his men to keep working. The British attacked later that morning.

The militia were told not to fire until the British were very close. This was dangerous, but those brave Americans did it. The British marched up the hill to attack two times in a row, but Americans held their ground, forcing the British back down the hill both times. A third British attack finally worked because Americans had run out of gun powder.

The British technically won, but it felt like an American victory because they'd held off the British for so long.

Fun Fact Corner
- The British had more than 1000 casualties, but Americans had about 400.
- Legend has it that Americans on Breed's Hill were told: "Don't one of you fire until you see the whites of their eyes!"
- British General William Howe brought a bottle of wine into battle, thinking he would win easily and celebrate his success. The bottle broke instead.

To learn more about the Battle of Bunker Hill, turn to page 48.

★ The British Leave Boston ★

The British soldiers had been trapped in Boston for several months when one of George Washington's officers had an idea.

Americans had captured two forts in New York. Those forts had many cannons. If they were brought to Boston, they could be used to scare the British, and the British might finally leave in their boats.

The trip to get the cannon was very hard, but American Colonel Henry Knox was sure he could do it. He hired men, sleds, and oxen to help. Together, they dragged the cannon through snow, across icy lakes, and down steep hills.

Fun Fact Corner

- Knox brought 58 mortars and cannons from New York. The total weight of these weapons was at least 120,000 pounds. That's like trying to carry or drag 29 cars across ice and snow.
- One cannon broke through the ice in the Hudson River and sank. Knox managed to get it out of the water anyway.
- George Washington's army spent weeks building fortifications that they could drag up Dorchester Heights, along with the cannon. It was too much work for one night otherwise.

To learn more about Dorchester Heights, turn to page 49.

It took weeks, but they made it to Boston.

George Washington had a plan. He had his army drag the cannon up some hills close to Boston. They worked in the middle of the night while the British soldiers were sleeping. When the British woke up, they saw all the cannon overlooking the city. It was a huge surprise.

A few days later, the British got in their boats and left Boston. Americans had taken back their city.

★ The Declaration of Independence ★

While the British were trapped in Boston, the Continental Congress had been debating what to do next. Could they work things out with the King? Or should they declare America free from Great Britain?

They wrote a petition to the King and sent it across the ocean. They asked him to make things more fair, but the King refused. He wouldn't even read the petition when it arrived in Great Britain.

The delegates to Congress realized that Americans could not continue to be part of the British empire. God makes every person equal, and every person has the right to life, liberty, and the pursuit of happiness. The King and Parliament were ignoring these truths, so it was time to break free.

On July 4, Congress approved a Declaration of Independence. Americans would begin again with a new government that knows it's not the boss of its people. The people are the boss of government. This is still true today! We, as Americans, are the boss of our own government.

Fun Fact Corner

- Congress's petition to the King was called the Olive Branch Petition. Congressional members approved it on July 5, 1775, one year before the Declaration of Independence.

- Congress appointed a committee of five men to write the Declaration of Independence, but Thomas Jefferson wrote the first draft.

- Jefferson's first draft had strong language condemning slavery, but Congress took it out.

- Congress approved the concept of independence on July 2, 1776, but it did not approve the official document until July 4, 1776.

- John Adams thought we would celebrate July 2 as America's birthday, not July 4!

To learn more about the Declaration of Independence, turn to page 50.

⋆ The Battle of Long Island ⋆

While Congress debated independence, George Washington took his army from Boston to New York City. He was sure the British would go there next. He was right, but the British didn't come right away. First, they gathered a huge fleet of warships. More than 400 ships came together and waited near New York.

Then the British attacked. About 20,000 British soldiers got off the ships and began invading Long Island. Meanwhile, Washington had only about 9,000 soldiers. The two sides fought hard, but by the end of the day, Americans were trapped in a corner of Brooklyn.

Fun Fact Corner

- Washington received inaccurate reports about what the British were planning. He thought a small attack was coming at Long Island, but that the real attack would be bigger and in another part of New York.
- The fog was heavy by Brooklyn, but there was no fog on the other side of the river. It lifted shortly after the army had escaped. Washington would later say that a divine hand had intervened for Americans during the war.

To learn more about the Battle of Long Island, turn to page 51.

The British army was in front of Washington's soldiers, but the East River was behind them. British ships were still floating nearby, so Americans would have trouble crossing the river without being seen.

The British were about to win. But then something amazing happened.

George Washington tricked the British. He told some of his men to build big campfires when night fell. They'd pretend they were staying.

No one noticed when the other soldiers began quietly getting in boats and sneaking across the East River in the middle of the night.

The Americans' escape took all night, and some soldiers were still waiting their turn when morning broke. Fortunately, a big fog came and settled over the area. It kept the British in the ships from seeing the Americans until everyone had safely escaped across the river.

★ Crossing the Delaware ★

George Washington and his army had escaped Brooklyn, but it wasn't long before the British were chasing them again. In fact, the British chased his army all the way across New York and New Jersey.

Americans were getting tired and discouraged. They weren't professional soldiers. They were just normal people who had left their lives behind so they could fight for freedom. Some of these men had promised to stay with Washington's army through New Year's Day, but then they planned to leave.

Washington knew he needed a big victory so the men would be encouraged and keep fighting. He decided to attack the British outpost at Trenton, New Jersey. The British had hired German soldiers, called Hessians, to watch the outpost, but the Hessians had hunkered down for the icy weather. It would be easy to surprise them.

Washington and his men would have to make a dangerous trip across the icy Delaware River. They would go on Christmas night. Then they would attack early in the morning.

It worked! The Hessians were taken off guard, and the battle was over in less than 45 minutes. George Washington had won an astonishing victory, just when he needed it most.

Fun Fact Corner

- Washington sent three groups of soldiers across the river, but the trip was so hard that two groups turned around. Washington's group made it.
- A winter storm hit just as Americans began crossing the river. It made the crossing much more difficult, but it also hid any noise the Americans made.
- The swirling snow mixed with gunpowder smoke confused the Hessians, keeping them from mounting a good defense.

To learn more about the Delaware Crossing, turn to page 51.

★ Victory at Saratoga ★

The British needed a new plan for stopping the American Revolution, so they sent one of their generals to lead soldiers from Canada down through the Hudson River Valley in New York. They hoped to separate the northeastern colonies from the others.

It didn't go too well for the British. They won some victories and captured a fort, but they also ran into trouble when Americans blocked roads or destroyed bridges that the British needed.

Fun Fact Corner

- Americans at Saratoga were led by one of George Washington's generals: Horatio Gates. Washington was with a different part of the army; he was fighting battles in Pennsylvania.
- The British in New York were led by General John Burgoyne. The British in Pennsylvania were led by General William Howe.
- Saratoga was technically two battles, with the first in September and the second in October. Burgoyne surrendered on October 17, 1777.
- The victory at Saratoga helped convince France to ally with the American colonies. French help made a big difference: They provided arms and ammunition as well as military support on the ground and at sea.

To learn more about Saratoga, turn to page 52.

Finally, the two sides met near Saratoga, New York.

The battle that followed was huge and took more than one day. British officers thought Americans fought with courage—even stubbornness. Americans simply refused to give up.

One American officer later said this was because his men had more at stake than a soldiers' salary. They were fighting for freedom!

Americans finally captured some British defenses, so the British tried to retreat. They couldn't get away, though, and had to surrender.

Americans had won another stunning victory!

⭐ Winter in Valley Forge ⭐

Americans had been fighting in both New York and Pennsylvania, but now winter was coming again. The British had captured Philadelphia and made winter camp there. George Washington wasn't so lucky. He and his men made camp at a place called Valley Forge, near Philadelphia.

It was very cold, and there were big snowstorms. Sometimes, Washington didn't have enough food or supplies. Some of the men didn't have enough clothes to keep warm, and many people got sick.

The winter was very hard, and people sometimes talk about the bad parts of Valley Forge, but there were good parts, too.

Fun Fact Corner

- The Oneida Indians came to help Washington's army during the long winter at Valley Forge. They brought white corn and tribe member Polly Cooper taught the Americans how to cook it.
- George Washington wintered with his troops because he did not go home for most of the war. He left Mount Vernon in 1775 and did not return until 1781.
- Von Steuben wrote his drills for the army in French because he didn't speak English. His secretary translated them.

To learn more about Valley Forge, turn to page 53.

The men kept busy, building huts to sleep in. They helped each other and worked as a team. For instance, the men who had more clothes took the outdoor tasks so those with less warm clothing could stay inside.

Washington also got good news when a Prussian officer arrived to help partway through the winter. Baron von Steuben knew army drills, and he taught Washington's men many tricks to be better soldiers.

Finally, the army got help when a group of men came from Congress. They talked to General Washington, and they worked out ways for Congress to do a better job of supporting the army.

The winter was long and hard, but Washington and his men persevered. They came out of winter camp a stronger and tougher army, ready to fight the British once more.

★ George Washington at Monmouth ★

Winter was over, so the British army left Philadelphia, and George Washington left Valley Forge to chase them. The two sides met in battle at Monmouth Court House in New Jersey.

One of Washington's officers, Charles Lee, was the first to run into British soldiers. He'd been leading a small group of Americans that was supposed to go ahead of Washington's main army.

Lee did a terrible job. The battle was going badly for Americans, and Lee ordered a retreat.

Just then, Washington arrived. He couldn't believe his eyes. Why was Lee telling his men to run away?

Fun Fact Corner

- Americans were chasing the British after Valley Forge, but they kept wondering why the British weren't moving faster. Was it a trick?
- As a young man, George Washington struggled to learn to control his temper. He became very good at it, overall, but Lee's retreat at Monmouth was one of the few times that his soldiers saw him lose his temper.
- Charles Lee thought he should have been Commander-in-Chief, instead of George Washington.

To learn more about the Battle of Monmouth, turn to page 54.

Washington took charge. He turned everyone back around, and they began a very tough battle against the British. It was incredibly hot outside, but Washington's army persevered for the whole day.

Everyone went to bed, and Washington thought the battle would start again the next morning. But when he woke up, he discovered that the British had run away in the middle of the night.

It was the first battle Americans fought after their training at Valley Forge. They were already doing better.

★ Southern Colonies Attacked ★

The Revolution had been going on for more than three years when George Washington won his victory at Monmouth. During that time, most of the big battles had been fought in the northern colonies.

The British could see that it wasn't working. Washington won some amazing victories—and he managed to escape when he was losing.

The British needed a new strategy, so they decided to start fighting more in the South. Things got very bad for the Americans after that.

In late 1778, the British captured Savannah, Georgia. Then they captured Augusta, also in Georgia, before moving on to Charleston and Camden, in South Carolina.

There was one very bad battle called the Battle of Waxhaws. Americans laid down their arms and offered to be taken prisoner, but the British refused.

This went on for most of two years. Americans could have given up on the fight for freedom, but they didn't.

Fun Fact Corner

- The Continental Army in the South had three leaders: Benjamin Lincoln, Horatio Gates, and Nathanael Greene.
- Nathanael Greene was called "The Fighting Quaker." He arrived in the South in late 1780, and things began to turn around after that.
- Some battles were fought by regular Continental and British soldiers, but many others were fought by militia. It felt like a civil war between colonists who wanted independence (Patriots) and those who did not (Loyalists).
- During part of this time, George Washington was in the North dealing with something unexpected: A trusted officer, Benedict Arnold, had turned traitor and almost helped the British to seize a fort at West Point.

To learn more about the Revolution in the South, turn to page 55.

★ Americans Start Winning ★

By this time, the war was in its sixth year. Can you imagine fighting for so long, without giving up? What a relief when Americans finally won a big battle in the South.

The victory came because British Major Patrick Ferguson threatened southern colonists. He told them to quit fighting, or he'd destroy their homes and farms. He thought he'd scare people, but he didn't. Americans became even more determined.

Fun Fact Corner

- One important battle won by the colonists was the Battle of Cowpens. It's said that the Patriot militia gave the British a "devil of a whipping" there.
- Another important battle was at Guilford Courthouse. The British technically won, but it was like Bunker Hill: The British were so worn down afterwards that it felt like a victory.
- Some battles were still being fought in the North during this time, including attacks on Virginia and Connecticut. There was also an attempt to capture the then-Governor of Virginia, Thomas Jefferson.

To learn more about the Revolution in the South, turn to page 55.

Nine hundred militia attacked Ferguson and his 1,100 men at a place called King's Mountain. Americans fought hard and won a huge victory. It changed the mood in the South.

After that, Americans still weren't winning every battle, but it felt like they were winning more of the battles that mattered.

Of course, the biggest, most important victory would be won by George Washington, and that battle was just around the corner.

⭐ British Trapped in Yorktown ⭐

George Washington needed to make an important decision. New York had been the British headquarters for most of the war. Should he stay up north and attack New York? Or should he go south?

British General Charles Cornwallis was then in Yorktown, Virginia. Perhaps the British could be trapped there and forced to surrender.

Just then, Washington got some good news: A fleet of French ships would help him if he chose to go south. Washington turned towards Virginia, but he left behind a small group of soldiers. They would pretend to prepare for an attack on New York.

Fun Fact Corner

- The French ships fought a battle against some British ships before they arrived outside Yorktown. The French won that battle and the surviving British ships fled to New York. Cornwallis was left stranded and alone.
- George Washington was normally pretty restrained, but when he saw the French ships that had come to help, he reportedly waved his hat in the air, joyfully, and gave an officer standing next to him a big hug.

To learn more about the Battle of Yorktown, turn to page 56.

No one would know that Washington was headed to Virginia until it was too late.

Once in Virginia, Washington joined forces with local militia and soldiers already in the South. Together, they surrounded Yorktown on land. In the meantime, the French ships sat in the harbor outside Yorktown, surrounding the British by sea, too.

Cornwallis was trapped. He would stay there for three long weeks.

★ Americans Win the War ★

British General Cornwallis was surrounded at Yorktown, unable to get new food or supplies. He could only hold out for so long. After three weeks, he raised a white flag. He was ready to give up.

His surrender to George Washington meant that Americans had won the war. It was an incredible moment. No one had thought that Americans could win. They thought the British military was too powerful.

George Washington thought the American victory was nothing short of a miracle, and he asked his soldiers to thank God for their victory.

The American Revolution changed the world. Americans went on to create a new Constitution and a new type of country. "We the People" of the United States are in charge. Kings and Queens do not get to boss us around.

It all started with normal people—just like you. These Americans had enough of bossy Kings, and they decided to fight for freedom. Men and women, rich and poor, lawyers and farmers, northerners and southerners persevered, worked hard, and helped each other.

They believed they could accomplish the impossible—and then they did. Generations of Americans have been doing the same ever since.

Fun Fact Corner

- The American Revolution didn't officially end until the United States and Great Britain signed the Treaty of Paris on September 3, 1783.
- Treaty negotiations were difficult because the British didn't want to recognize the United States of America as a real country. They tried to recognize only individual colonies.

To learn more about the Battle of Yorktown, turn to page 56.

Timeline of the

Stamp Act Approved
March 22, 1765

Stamp Act Repealed
March 18, 1766

1765   1766   1767   1768   1769

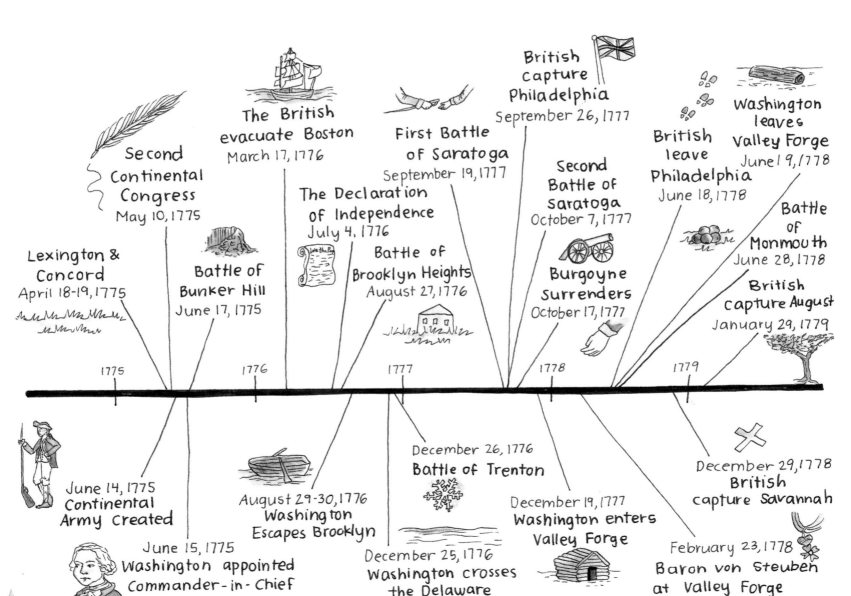

Second Continental Congress
May 10, 1775

The British evacuate Boston
March 17, 1776

First Battle of Saratoga
September 19, 1777

British capture Philadelphia
September 26, 1777

British leave Philadelphia
June 18, 1778

Washington leaves Valley Forge
June 19, 1778

The Declaration of Independence
July 4, 1776

Second Battle of Saratoga
October 7, 1777

Lexington & Concord
April 18-19, 1775

Battle of Bunker Hill
June 17, 1775

Battle of Brooklyn Heights
August 27, 1776

Burgoyne Surrenders
October 17, 1777

Battle of Monmouth
June 28, 1778

British capture August
January 29, 1779

1775   1776   1777   1778   1779

June 14, 1775
Continental Army Created

August 29-30, 1776
Washington Escapes Brooklyn

December 26, 1776
Battle of Trenton

December 29, 1778
British capture Savannah

June 15, 1775
Washington appointed Commander-in-Chief

December 25, 1776
Washington crosses the Delaware

December 19, 1777
Washington enters Valley Forge

February 23, 1778
Baron von Steuben at Valley Forge

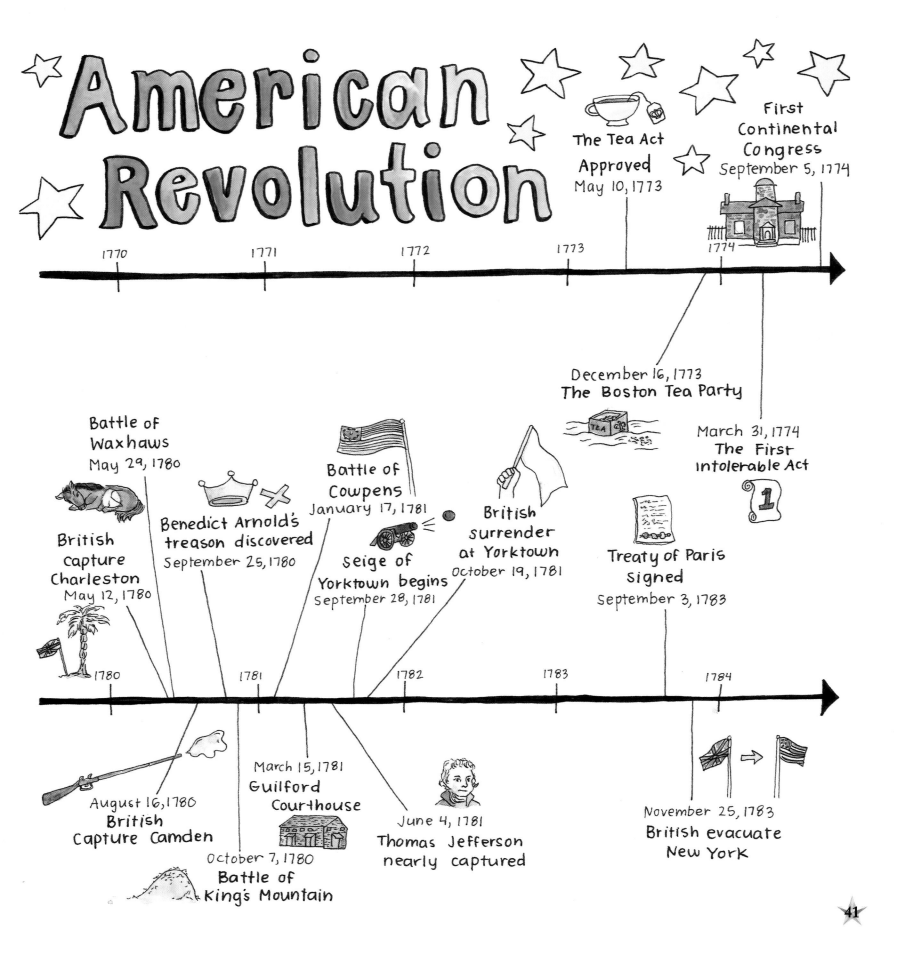

American Revolution

The Tea Act Approved
May 10, 1773

First Continental Congress
September 5, 1774

1770   1771   1772   1773   1774

December 16, 1773
The Boston Tea Party

March 31, 1774
The First Intolerable Act

Battle of Waxhaws
May 29, 1780

Benedict Arnold's treason discovered
September 25, 1780

Battle of Cowpens
January 17, 1781

British surrender at Yorktown
October 19, 1781

Siege of Yorktown begins
September 28, 1781

Treaty of Paris Signed
September 3, 1783

British capture Charleston
May 12, 1780

1780   1781   1782   1783   1784

August 16, 1780
British Capture Camden

March 15, 1781
Guilford Courthouse

June 4, 1781
Thomas Jefferson nearly captured

November 25, 1783
British evacuate New York

October 7, 1780
Battle of King's Mountain

41

✦ Notes and Sources ✦

Stamp Act: The Stamp Act was approved in March 1765, but it didn't go into effect right away. Thus, colonists had months in which to stew over the injustice: Why should Parliament be allowed to tax Americans when they had no representation in that body?! This encroachment upon their rights would not stand. Mobs burned the effigies of stamp collectors and Royal Governors. British goods were boycotted. A Stamp Act Congress sent a Declaration of Rights and Grievances to the King. "The People, even to the lowest Ranks," John Adams wrote, "have become more attentive to their Liberties, more inquisitive about them, and more determined to defend them, than they were ever before known or had occasion to be." On November 1, when the tax went into effect, no stamps were sold in the colonies, except for a few in Georgia. "IF you comply with the Act, by using Stamped Papers," a broadside blared, "you fix, you rivet perpetual Chains upon your unhappy Country . . . . If you quietly bend your Necks to that Yoke, you prove yourselves ready to receive any Bondage to which your *Lords* and *Masters* shall please to subject you." One parliamentary member declared: "I rejoice that America has resisted. Three million of people so dead to all feelings of liberty, as voluntarily to submit to be slaves, would have been fit instruments to make slaves of the rest." Parliament repealed the Stamp Act but also resolved that it had "full power and authority" to make laws "to bind the colonies and people of America, subjects of the crown of Great Britain, in all cases whatsoever." The colonists didn't notice that Parliament had reserved the right to tax them again. Instead, boycotts were dropped, and the colonists celebrated their victory.

Sources & Further Reading: David F. Burg, The American Revolution (updated ed. 2007); Edmund S. Morgan & Helen M. Morgan, The Stamp Act Crisis: Prologue to Revolution (1995); John Adams, Diary entry (Dec. 18, 1765), *in* 1 The Adams Papers: Diary and Autobiography of John Adams 263-65 (L. H. Butterfield et al. eds., 1961); The Declaratory Act (March 18, 1766) (Gr. Brit.); William Pitt, Speech on the Stamp Act (Jan. 14, 1766), *in* Speeches that Changed the World 111-15 (Owen Collins ed., Westminster John Knox Press 1999) (1998).

Boston Tea Party: Contrary to popular mythology, Americans were already paying taxes on tea prior to the Boston Tea Party. They'd been paying those taxes since 1767, when the British Parliament enacted a variety of new taxes through the Townshend Acts. Those taxes created a huge furor in the colonies, and Parliament ultimately repealed most of them. Yet the tax on tea stayed. Years later, Parliament enacted the Tea Act of 1773. That Act did not create any new taxes on tea. To the contrary, the Act made tea cheaper because it eliminated middlemen and generally made things easier for the British East India Company. (Parliament was trying to bail the company out; it had 17 million pounds of surplus tea.) The colonists did not think the taxes on tea were legitimate in the first place, and they had no intention of now paying taxes on what had become a forced monopoly. The first load of tea arrived in Boston Harbor in late November, with two other boatloads soon following. Taxes on tea were due within 20 days of a ship arriving in harbor. Boston residents wanted to reject the shipments, but the Loyalist governor refused. The colonists were irate and held multiple town hall-type meetings. A subset of the colonists, the Sons of Liberty, hatched a secret plan. On the night of December 16, more than 100 men dressed up as American Indians. They boarded the ships and threw 46 tons of tea into the harbor. When they were done, the protestors returned home. "This is the most magnificent Movement of all," future President John Adams wrote. "There is a Dignity, a Majesty, a Sublimity, in this last Effort of the Patriots, that I greatly admire.... This Destruction of the Tea is so bold, so daring, so firm, intrepid and inflexible, and it must have so important Consequences, and so lasting, that I cant but consider it as an Epocha in History."

Sources & Further Reading: Boston Tea Party History, Boston Tea Party Ships & Museum (last visited June 2, 2022), https://www.bostonteapartyship.com/boston-tea-party-history; Harlow Giles Unger, American Tempest: How the Boston Tea Party Sparked a Revolution (2011); John Adams, Diary entry (Dec. 17, 1773), *in* 2 The Adams Papers: Diary and Autobiography of John Adams 85-87 (L. H. Butterfield et al. eds., 1962).

Intolerable Acts: Parliament punished Bostonians in the wake of their Tea Party with a series of measures that came to be known as the "Intolerable Acts." The first, the Boston Port Act, closed the city's port until reimbursement for the tea was made. Other, similar measures followed. British soldiers were sent to Massachusetts to enforce the new laws, but Bostonians soon sent a circular letter to their sister colonies: "This Attack, though made immediately upon us, is doubtless design'd for every other Colony, who will not surrender their sacred Rights & Liberties . . . . be assured, *you* will be called upon to surrender your Rights, if ever they should succeed in their Attempts to suppress the Spirit of Liberty *here*." A Continental Congress was called. Every colony (except Georgia) sent delegates so they could define terms for a boycott of British goods. Interestingly, that Congress was confronted with a question that has cropped up repeatedly in America: How can large and small colonies fairly work together in one union? Large colony delegates wanted more votes, but one small colony delegate "observed that a little Colony had its All at Stake as well as a great one." In the end, each colony, both large and small, was given one vote. Another thorny issue confronted delegates: Should Congress open with prayer? Some delegates worried "because we were so divided in religious Sentiments," but Samuel Adams declared that he "was no Bigot, and could hear a Prayer from a Gentleman of Piety and Virtue, who was at the same Time a Friend to his Country." The Reverend Jacob Duché opened with Psalm 35, the collect for the day. John Adams later marveled that it "seemed as if Heaven had ordained that Psalm to be read on that Morning." The Psalm begins: "Contend, Lord, with those who contend with me; fight against those who fight against me."

Sources & Further Reading: 1 DAVID RAMSAY, THE HISTORY OF THE AMERICAN REVOLUTION (1789); John Adams, Diary entry (Sept. 5, 1774), *in* 2 THE ADAMS PAPERS: DIARY AND AUTOBIOGRAPHY OF JOHN ADAMS 122-24 (L. H. Butterfield et al. eds., 1962); 1 JOURNALS OF THE CONTINENTAL CONGRESS, 1774-89, at 13-27 (Worthington Chauncey Ford ed., Government Printing Office 1904); Letter from John Adams to Abigail Adams (Sept. 16, 1774), *in* 1 THE ADAMS PAPERS: ADAMS FAMILY CORRESPONDENCE 156-57 (L. H. Butterfield et al. eds., 1963); The Committee of Correspondence of Boston to the Committee of Correspondence of Philadelphia (May 13, 1774), *in* 3 THE WRITINGS OF SAMUEL ADAMS 109-11 (Harry Alonzo Cushing ed., 1907).

Paul Revere's Ride: Massachusetts was in turmoil in early 1775. A Royal Governor had been appointed, British soldiers patrolled Boston—and Patriots had formed a secret committee to keep an eye on these soldiers. One Patriot leader, Dr. Joseph Warren, sent for Paul Revere late on April 18. He asked Revere to ride to Lexington, carrying a warning for John Hancock and Samuel

Adams. It was believed they were about to be arrested. The ride was risky, and another man, William Dawes, had already been dispatched with the same message. The hope was that one of the two messengers would arrive safely. A signaling system had also been pre-arranged: If the British were coming "by Water, we would shew two Lanthorns in the North Church Steeple; & if by Land, one, as a Signal." Revere ensured that someone would send this signal, then two friends rowed him across the Charles River. He took off on horseback. By his own account, he soon "saw two men on Horse back, under a Tree. When I got near them, I discovered they were British officer. One tryed to git a head of Me, & the other to take me. I turned my Horse . . . . I got clear of him . . . ." Revere arrived at Lexington with his warning for Hancock and Adams, then he and Dawes continued on to Concord. They were joined by Dr. Samuel Prescott, but the trio was soon stopped by British officers. Prescott and Dawes escaped; Revere did not. One officer, Revere wrote, "Clapped his pistol to my head, called me by name, & told me he was going to ask me some questions, & if I did not give him true answers, he would blow my brains out." Revere got away when the soldiers heard shots fired at Lexington. "[T]he Major asked what that was for," Revere later testified. "I told him to alarm the Country." The British took Revere's horse and left. While Revere was a prisoner, Prescott delivered the warning to Concord.

Sources & Further Reading: Fischer, *infra* page 57; Henry W. Longfellow, Paul Revere's Ride (1905); Letter from Paul Revere to Jeremy Belknap (1798), https://www.masshist.org/database/99 (last visited June 2, 2022); Paul Revere's draft deposition (circa 1775), https://www.masshist.org/database/97 (last visited June 2, 2022); Philbrick, *infra* page 57.

Lexington and Concord: Roughly 700 British soldiers began marching towards Concord on the same night that Paul Revere made his famous ride. The soldiers were supposed to seize the colonists' weapons and supplies. Instead, they ran into about 70 American minutemen on Lexington Green early on April 19. Someone heard a British officer shout: "Lay down your arms, you damned rebels!" Others heard similar statements: "Throw down your arms, ye villains, ye rebels" or "Ye villains, ye rebels, disperse, damn you, disperse!" One American officer later testified that he "immediately ordered our Militia to disperse, and not to fire." Some did, but others never heard the order—and **none** of the Americans put down their arms. No one knows who fired the first shot. Some British officers were certain that it was a provincial hidden behind a hedge. Others thought the shot came from a nearby tavern. Some militia were certain that British officers fired first. Either way, the first shot **was** fired. The British began firing at Americans, leaving 18 Americans killed or wounded. Only a few Americans returned fire, so only one British soldier was mildly wounded. The British continued toward Concord. They couldn't find any weapons there and might have returned peacefully to Boston but for one thing: A fire broke out, and some militia thought the British were burning down the town. A brief skirmish ensued, but then the British retreated towards Boston, with Americans firing on them the whole way. In all, nearly 300 British soldiers were killed or wounded during the retreat. Americans lost less than 100. The day ended with the British under siege in Boston.

Sources & Further Reading: Fischer, *infra* page 57; 2 Journals of the Continental Congress, 1774-89, at 28-44 (Worthington Chauncey Ford ed., Government Printing Office 1905); Philbrick, *infra* page 57.

General George Washington: The siege of Boston was initially handled by a conglomeration of New England militia, without any real authority structure or stable source of supplies. The lack of structure made the men defiant and unruly. John Adams, then a delegate in the Continental Congress, advocated for a solution: the creation of a new, Continental Army. On June 14, 1775, Congress did just that, voting to raise multiple companies of riflemen who were to "march and join the army near Boston." Congress then turned to the question of who should lead this army. John Adams had an idea for that, too. He spoke to Congress of a "Gentleman from Virginia who was among Us." This man, Adams concluded, "would command the Approbation of all America, and unite the cordial Exertions of all the Colonies better than any other…." He did not mention George Washington by name, but everyone understood the reference. Adams related that Washington, "as soon as he heard me allude to him, from his Usual Modesty darted into the Library Room." Congress appointed Washington as Commander-in-Chief the next day. Washington accepted humbly, noting the "high Honour done me, in this Appointment, yet I feel great distress, from a consciousness that my abilities & Military experience may not be equal to the extensive & important Trust." One of his few surviving letters to Martha Washington expresses similar sentiments. He wrote: "You may beleive me my dear . . . I have used every endeavour in my power to avoid [the appointment], not only from my unwillingness to part with you and the Family, but from a consciousness of its being a trust too great for my Capacity and that I should enjoy more real happiness and felicity in one month with you, at home . . . ." In the end, Washington served. He was never one to shirk a call to duty.

Sources & Further Reading: 4 Douglas Southall Freeman, George Washington, A Biography: Leader of the Revolution (1951); Edward G. Lengel, General George Washington: A Military Life (2005); George Washington, Address to the Continental Congress (June 16, 1775), *in* 1 The Papers of George Washington: Revolutionary War Series 1-3 (W.W. Abbot et al. eds., 1985) [hereinafter War Series]; John Adams, *In Congress, June and July 1775, in* 3 The Adams Papers: Diary and Autobiography of John Adams 322-24 (L. H. Butterfield et al. eds., 1962); 2 Journals of the Continental Congress, 1774-89, at 89-95 (Worthington Chauncey Ford ed., Government Printing Office 1905); Letter from George Washington to Martha Washington (June 18, 1775), *in* 1 War Series, *supra*, 3-5.

Battle of Bunker Hill: American Colonel William Prescott undertook a midnight mission to fortify Bunker Hill during the siege of Boston. Americans wanted to shore up their defenses outside the city, but they also wanted to do it secretly, while the British slept. Unfortunately, Prescott's group ended up fortifying the wrong hill—Breed's Hill—as it worked in the dead of night. Was it a mistake? Or did he intentionally bypass Bunker Hill and go to Breed's Hill? No one really knows. Nevertheless, the decision had consequences. Breed's Hill was closer to Boston than was Bunker Hill. Thus, fortifying it was "an unmistakable act of defiance" that "invited a forceful response from the British army," historian Nathaniel Philbrick notes. Adding to the mystery of Prescott's actions, Bunker Hill already had partially completed defenses, and it would have been quicker to finish those fortifications than to start anew on Breed's Hill. Perhaps unsurprisingly, Americans could not complete the fortifications before sunrise and discovery by the British. The next morning, the British first bombarded, then marched on, the American position. At least apocryphally, the American militia were told: "Don't one of you fire until you see the whites of their eyes!" Those precise words probably weren't uttered, but one American officer may have said not to fire until the British soldiers' white gaiters (leg coverings) were visible. Either way, Americans held their fire. As a result, the British were very close to the Americans when the first barrage of musket fire came. It took down many British soldiers. A second attack met with the same result. The third attack went better for the British, partly because they had reorganized and partly because Americans were running out of gunpowder. The eventual British victory was costly: They'd lost more than twice as many men as the Americans. "I wish [we] could Sell them another Hill at the same Price," American General Nathanael Greene wrote.

Sources & Further Reading: FERLING, *infra* page 57; PHILBRICK, *infra* page 57; RICHARD FROTHINGHAM, HISTORY OF THE SIEGE OF BOSTON: AND THE BATTLES OF LEXINGTON, CONCORD, AND BUNKER HILL (4th ed. 1873); RICHARD M. KETCHUM, DECISIVE DAY: THE BATTLE FOR BUNKER HILL (1962).

Dorchester Heights: The British were under siege in Boston from April 1775 to March 1776. They might have stayed longer but for American Colonel Henry Knox. He'd had an idea: Why not retrieve cannons and artillery that could be found at Forts Ticonderoga and Crown Point and bring them to Boston? The cannons were available, but the forts were hundreds of miles away, in New York. It was winter and travel would be rough, but George Washington trusted Knox to finish the mission. Knox arrived at Fort Ticonderoga in early December 1775. He planned to ship the cannons down Lake George before beginning the difficult trip overland: nearly 300 miles. He hired men to help, but ice and rough winds complicated the voyage across the lake. More problems arose after they came ashore. Knox had arranged for sleds and oxen to haul the cannons, thinking that there would be snow. But there was no snow—at first. Then there was a blizzard and *too much* snow! At another point in the journey, the men had to get the heavy cannons down steep hills: They tethered the cannons to trees and slowly inched them down. Against all odds, Knox—and the cannon—reached Washington's army several weeks after they started. The cannons changed everything. Washington would use them to occupy and fortify Dorchester Heights, overlooking Boston. The move put British lines within range of the new American cannons. Washington determined to accomplish this feat in the middle of the night. Thus, on the morning of March 5, the British awoke to a surprising sight: American cannons were now staring down at them from the newly fortified Heights. On March 17, 1776, the British finally evacuated Boston, restoring the city to American control. It was an astounding victory for the newly appointed Washington.

Sources & Further Reading: George Washington's Instructions to Colonel Henry Knox (Nov. 16, 1775), *in* 2 The Papers of George Washington: Revolutionary War Series 384-85 (W.W. Abbot et al. eds., 1987) [hereinafter War Series]; Letter from Colonel Henry Knox to George Washington (Dec. 17, 1775), *in* 2 War Series, *supra*, at 563-65; Mark Puls, Henry Knox: Visionary General of the American Revolution (2008); McCullough, *infra* page 57.

Declaration of Independence: The Declaration of Independence was written by a Committee of Five (John Adams, Benjamin Franklin, Thomas Jefferson, Robert R. Livingston, and Roger Sherman), but Jefferson was the primary author of that document. His goal was not to write of "new principles, or new arguments, never before thought of." Instead, he wanted to "place before mankind the common sense of the subject; [in] terms so plain and firm, as to command their assent, and to justify ourselves in the independant stand we [are] compelled to take." He wanted it to be an "expression of the american mind." According to Adams, he and Jefferson met to discuss the first draft of the document. Adams later described himself as "delighted with its high tone, and the flights of Oratory with which it abounded." This initial draft contained a "vehement Phillipic against Negro Slavery," which also pleased Adams, although it was later struck. Jefferson's draft was presented to the Committee of Five, and some revisions were suggested. A draft was presented to Congress on June 28. Congress made more changes, but Adams felt that "they obliterated some of the best of it." Jefferson was also unhappy. He sent a copy of the original to fellow delegate Richard Henry Lee, who concurred that Congress had "mangled" the manuscript. However, Lee added cheerfully, "the *Thing* is in its nature so good, that no Cookery can spoil the Dish for the palates of Freemen." Once approved, news of the Declaration spread quickly. It was published in newspapers, read before towns, and forwarded to Europe. Mere days later, it was read aloud in Philadelphia, as the city's bells tolled to mark the event. There would be no more attempts to reconcile with Great Britain.

Sources & Further Reading: David McCullough, John Adams (2001); Joseph J. Ellis, Revolutionary Summer: The Birth of American Independence (2013); 5 Journals of the Continental Congress, 1774-89, at 431 & 491-516 (Worthington Chauncey Ford ed., Government Printing Office 1906); Pauline Maier, American Scripture: Making the Declaration of Independence (1997).

Battle of Long Island: George Washington was in New York during the summer of 1776. He knew an attack was coming because a massive fleet of warships had been gathering in the harbor outside the city for weeks. On the night of August 21, a violent thunderstorm struck, setting houses on fire and killing soldiers. When morning came, the British began an orderly invasion of Long Island. Eventually, about 20,000 British and Hessian troops came ashore. Meanwhile, Americans had about 9,000 soldiers in and around Brooklyn (the part of Long Island that is closest to Manhattan). The British made their next move on the night of August 26, silently marching 9 miles towards the Americans in the pitch dark. They attacked the next morning. Americans fought gallantly but were soon cornered in Brooklyn with the East River behind them. Washington was in a tough spot. He was with his soldiers in Brooklyn, but some of his army was still across the river in Manhattan. The Brooklyn half of the army was trapped, its ammunition ruined by a storm that had sprung up on August 28. Washington determined to escape across the East River, but he'd have to manage it without being seen by the British warships hovering nearby. At 7 p.m. on August 29, the troops were told to pack up. The least experienced troops, along with the sick and wounded, were ordered to the river first. The rain from the storm, however, had made the current so swift that a crossing was impossible. The first round of troops simply stood there until about 11:00 p.m., waiting. Finally, the river calmed enough for the boats to cross, but everything was moving too slowly. It must have seemed that all was lost until a sudden, heavy fog settled over Brooklyn. The last of Washington's men completed their escape across the river at about 7 a.m. The fog lifted shortly thereafter. Nine thousand men had crossed the river, all without being seen by the British. Washington's army had gone from crushing defeat to miraculous escape in a matter of days.

Sources & Further Reading: McCullough, *infra* page 57; Ron Chernow, Washington: A Life (2010); Steven H. Jaffe, New York at War: Four Centuries of Combat, Fear, and Intrigue in Gotham (2012).

Delaware Crossing: In late 1776, Washington's army was reeling from a series of crushing defeats: The British had won important battles in New York and had chased Americans across New Jersey. Winter had arrived, so British General William Howe decided to retire to New York

City. (Back then, armies did not typically expect to fight in tough winter weather.) Although he was leaving, Howe left several outposts behind in New Jersey to protect the ground he'd won. Meanwhile, Washington had roughly 6,000 men fit for duty, but many of those enlistments would end on New Year's Day. He needed to recruit new soldiers—or inspire the existing ones to stay. He and his officers planned a surprise attack: The army would cross the Delaware River in three different locations, and they'd hit the British outpost at Trenton, New Jersey, before sunrise. The army began its crossing on Christmas night. One officer, Henry Knox, would later describe the "almost infinite difficulty" created by the icy conditions. Making matters worse, a northeaster sprang up. Amazingly, Washington's group managed to cross the river—even getting horses and cannon across. Unfortunately, those in the other two crossings had deemed it too difficult and turned back. Washington and his men, however, pushed on relentlessly, through snow and ice, finally reaching Trenton about three hours later than planned. The storms turned out to be both a blessing and a curse that night. The snow and ice made the crossing almost impossible, but they also kept the 1,500 Hessians stationed at Trenton from realizing that an attack was under way until it was too late. Americans were tired, wet, and cold, but they attacked just after 8 a.m. and fought gallantly. Things were happening quickly. Snow and gunpowder smoke swirled around and confused the Hessians, who tried (and failed) to retreat before surrendering. Washington had won a stunning victory just when it was needed most.

Sources & Further Reading: DAVID HACKETT FISCHER, WASHINGTON'S CROSSING (2004); FERLING, *infra* page 57; LENGEL, *infra* page 57; McCULLOUGH, *infra* page 57.

Saratoga: British Lt. General John Burgoyne had a mission during the summer of 1777: He was to travel from Canada down to Albany in an attempt to separate the New England colonies from the southern ones. Burgoyne started off well, with an easy capture of Ft. Ticonderoga, but then his campaign took a turn for the worse. He had trouble getting supplies. Anticipated reinforcements never came. Americans destroyed bridges, felled trees, and blocked roads in his path. He lost men at the Battle of Bennington and a first Battle of Saratoga. The latter battle was technically a British victory, but Burgoyne lost more men than had American General Horatio Gates. He also failed to drive Americans from a fortified position on Bemis Heights. Gates's army was growing larger as militia poured in, buoyed by the news. Burgoyne was in a bind. On October 7, he sent a "reconnaissance-in-force" of roughly 2,000 men, armed with cannons, toward the Americans. Gates dispatched two brigades, along with Daniel Morgan's riflemen to confront them. "True to his purpose," one observer described, "Morgan at this critical moment poured down like a torrent from the hill, and attacked the right of the enemy in front and flank." The British were soon in full retreat, but Americans pursued and surrounded Burgoyne. The British general formally surrendered on October 17.

Sources & Further Reading: JOHN LUZADER, SARATOGA: A MILITARY HISTORY OF THE DECISIVE CAMPAIGN OF THE AMERICAN REVOLUTION (2008); KETCHUM, *infra* page 57; NATHANIEL PHILBRICK, VALIANT AMBITION: GEORGE WASHINGTON, BENEDICT ARNOLD, AND THE FATE OF THE AMERICAN REVOLUTION (2016).

Valley Forge: George Washington's army spent the winter of 1777-78 in Valley Forge, outside Philadelphia. (The city itself was then in the hands of the British.) History books often talk about the cold, sickness, and lack of supplies at Valley Forge. Those things happened, but there were good things, too, and the mood was significantly better than you might imagine. Everyone pitched in, finding supplies and building huts. "The sound that would have reached your ears on approaching the camp was not that of a forlorn howling wind," the National Park Service notes, "but rather that of hammers, axes, saws, and shovels at work." Meanwhile, Washington used the time productively: He met with a congressional delegation, seeking much-needed reforms. He also obtained the help of a former Prussian officer, Baron von Steuben, who'd come to America with a letter of introduction from Benjamin Franklin. The Prussian taught the men, and he created a drill manual. (This "Blue Book" became the first manual for the United States Army and remained in use until 1812.) The winter at Valley Forge was long, of course. Some died from flu, typhus, and other diseases. Yet, at the same time, the army improved, and it emerged from its winter encampment better able to fight the British.

Sources & Further Reading: Eyewitness account of Chevalier de Pontgibaud, *in* THE HERITAGE OF AMERICA 168 (Henry Steele Commager & Allan Nevins eds., 1939); LENGEL, *infra* page 57; ROBERT K. WRIGHT, JR.,

CTR. OF MILITARY HIST., U.S. ARMY, THE CONTINENTAL ARMY (1983); *Skilled and Capable*, VALLEY FORGE NAT'L HIST. PARK, http://npshistory.com/publications/vafo/index.htm (last visited June 3, 2022); THOMAS FLEMING, WASHINGTON'S SERCRET WAR: THE HIDDEN HISTORY OF VALLEY FORGE (2005).

Battle of Monmouth: The clash at Monmouth occurred after Washington's army emerged from its long winter at Valley Forge. Americans were then in pursuit of the British, who'd just evacuated Philadelphia. On June 24, Washington held a council of war to discuss next steps. Most of his officers were reluctant to risk a full-fledged battle. The French had just agreed to help the American effort. Wouldn't it be prudent to avoid general engagements until after their arrival? Smaller harassing actions seemed more appropriate. One officer was especially adamant on this point: General Charles Lee. Unfortunately, Lee commanded the advance force that Washington later sent to harass the British rear guard. Lee moved against the British on June 28. "Much of what unfolded was disorderly," historian John Ferling reports, "due in no small measure to the conduct of the officers." Before too long, miscommunication among American officers had prompted a general retreat of Lee's forces. Washington later wrote of his "great surprize and mortification" when he discovered the "whole advanced Corps retreating, and, as I was told, by General Lee's orders without having made any opposition, except one fire . . . ." Lee and Washington exchanged sharp words. A private later wrote that Washington was "in a great passion," while one of the officers reported that Washington "swore that day till the leaves shook on the trees." (Washington lost his temper, but the allegation that he swore may be exaggerated; Washington didn't generally swear.) Either way, Washington assumed command and turned the retreat around. The battle continued for the rest of that painfully hot day, then both armies retired for the evening. At dawn, Washington made a startling discovery: The British had departed, silently, in the middle of the night. Americans declared victory because they retained the field. American forces, fresh from training at Valley Forge, had held their own against the British!

Sources & Further Reading: FERLING, *infra* page 57; Letter from George Washington to Henry Laurens (July 1, 1778), *in* 16 THE PAPERS OF GEORGE WASHINGTON: REVOLUTIONARY WAR SERIES 2-6 (Theodore J. Crackel et al. eds., 2006); MARK EDWARD LENDER & GARRY WHEELER STONE, FATAL SUNDAY: GEORGE WASHINGTON, THE MONMOUTH CAMPAIGN, AND THE POLITICS OF BATTLE (2016); PETER R. HENRIQUES, FIRST AND

Revolution in the South: The war in the North stalled after the American victory at Saratoga. The British needed a new strategy, so they turned to the South. They hoped to build a base there, then use that base to crush the rebellion in the North. The strategy worked at first. Americans lost an important port—Savannah, Georgia—late in 1778, then suffered another loss at Augusta, Georgia. The British abandoned Augusta after only a few weeks, but an American attempt to re-take Savannah failed. One especially bad moment came in South Carolina in May 1780: British Lt. Colonel Banastre Tarleton caught up with some American soldiers and won the bloody Battle of Waxhaws that followed. At about the same time, American Major General Benjamin Lincoln surrendered his entire force at Charleston, South Carolina. His replacement as commander of the southern army, American Major General Horatio Gates, lasted only a few weeks. In August 1780, Gates suffered a humiliating defeat at Camden, South Carolina. Fortunately, American (Patriot) militia began winning smaller victories, and these victories inspired Americans to keep fighting. The tide began to turn at King's Mountain, in South Carolina, in October 1780: A band of Patriot militia routed some colonial militia who were loyal to the King (Loyalists). Several weeks later, American Major General Nathanael Greene assumed command of the southern army. "We fight get beat rise and fight again," Greene said. "The whole Country is one continued scene of blood and slaughter." American soldiers and Patriot militia were succeeding more often. Southern militia leaders such as Frances Marion (the "Swamp Fox") engaged in guerilla warfare that kept the British off guard. Militia led by Daniel Morgan trounced the much-hated "Bloody Ban" Tarleton at Cowpens, in South Carolina. The southern arm of the Continental Army, led by Greene, enticed British General Charles Cornwallis deep into North Carolina, further and further from his supply lines. The British were getting worn down. A March 1781 battle at Guilford Court House was technically a British victory, but British casualties were so high that it felt like an American one. By September 1781, the British had been driven back into their bases at Charleston and Savannah. Cornwallis was in Yorktown, Virginia. The scene was set for the final American victory.

Sources & Further Reading: BUCHANAN, *infra* page 57; HENRY LUMPKIN, FROM SAVANNAH TO YORKTOWN: THE AMERICAN REVOLUTION IN THE SOUTH (1987); JOHN OLLER, THE SWAMP FOX: HOW FRANCIS MARION SAVED THE AMERICAN REVOLUTION (2016); LAWRENCE E. BABITS, A DEVIL OF A WHIPPING: THE BATTLE OF COWPENS (1998).

Battle of Yorktown: As the summer of 1781 closed, George Washington was working with his French allies and contemplating his next move: Should he attack the British in Yorktown or New York? Just then, Washington received some good news: French Admiral François Joseph Paul de Grasse was on his way, with as many as 29 ships. The Admiral was disinclined to travel as far as New York, but he could help further south. Washington asked the Marquis de Lafayette, already in the South, to contain British General Charles Cornwallis at Yorktown. French and American forces would head that way. Washington did not then know it, but his plan could have been foiled right from the beginning: De Grasse met British ships in a naval battle on September 5. What if he'd lost? Those British ships were outnumbered, though, and their commanders were doing a poor job. The British ultimately retreated, leaving Cornwallis alone in Yorktown, with no naval reinforcements. By September 28, American and French army and naval forces had Yorktown surrounded. Cornwallis finally surrendered after a three-week siege. Americans had won an impossible victory, and Washington credited God. "Divine Service is to be performed tomorrow in the several Brigades or Divisions," Washington ordered. "The Commander in Chief earnestly recommends that the troops not on duty should universally attend with that seriousness of Deportment and gratitude of Heart which the recognition of such reiterated and astonishing interpositions of Providence demand of us."

Sources & Further Reading: FERLING, *infra* page 57; General Orders (Oct. 20, 1781), *in* 23 THE WRITINGS OF GEORGE WASHINGTON FROM THE ORIGINAL MANUSCRIPT SOURCES 1745-1799, at 244-47 (John C. Fitzpatrick ed., 1937); JAMES THOMAS FLEXNER, WASHINGTON: THE INDISPENSABLE MAN (Back Bay ed. 1994); JOSEPH ELLIS, HIS EXCELLENCY: GEORGE WASHINGTON (2004).

✦ Other Resources ✦

Books for Adults

David Hackett Fischer, Paul Revere's Ride (1994)

David McCullough, 1776 (2005)

Edward G. Lengel, General George Washington: A Military Life (2005)

John Buchanan, The Road to Guilford Courthouse: The American Revolution in the Carolinas (1997)

John Ferling, Almost a Miracle: The American Victory in the War of Independence (2007)

Nathaniel Philbrick, Bunker Hill: A City, A Siege, A Revolution (2013)

Richard M. Ketchum, Saratoga: Turning Point of America's Revolutionary War (1997)

Rick Atkinson, The British Are Coming: The War for America, Lexington to Princeton, 1775-1777 (2019)

Books for Younger Readers

Lynne Cheney, When Washington Crossed the Delaware: A Wintertime Story for Young Patriots (2004)

Nathan Hale, One Dead Spy: A Revolutionary War Tale (2012)

Rush Revere and the American Revolution: Time-Travel Adventures with Exceptional Americans (2014)

Stephen Krensky, Dangerous Crossing: The Revolutionary Voyage of John Quincy Adams (2004)

Steve Sheinkin, King George: What Was His Problem?: Everything Your Schoolbooks Didn't Tell You About the American Revolution (2015)